WORDS *of* HOPE *and* HEALING

THE
GUILT
of GRIEF

How to Understand, Embrace,
and Restoratively Express
Guilt and Regret after a Loss

Alan D. Wolfelt, Ph.D.

Companion
P R E S S

An imprint of the Center for Loss and Life Transition | Fort Collins, Colorado

Companion Press is an imprint of the Center for Loss and Life Transition, 3735 Broken Bow Road, Fort Collins, Colorado 80526.

27   26   25   24   23   22   6 5 4 3 2 1

ISBN: 978-1-61722-315-0

CONTENTS

Welcome 1

    My Guilt, Shame, and Regret 2

Guilt, Shame, and Regret 5

    Judgment 5

    Backward-looking 6

    Secrecy 7

    Healing in Grief 8

    Guilt, Shame, or Regret? 9

    Clean Guilt Versus Dirty Guilt 13

    Types of Guilt 15

Understanding Your Guilt 19

    The Wolfelt Guilt Inventory 19

    Contributors to Guilt in Grief 23

    To Err Is Human 29

    The Utility of Grief 30

    The Dangers of Guilt 30

Befriending Your Guilt, Shame, and Regret 35

    Safety First 36

One Dose at a Time 36

The Intention of Befriending 37

The Mindfulness of Befriending. 38

Befriending Your Guilt 39

Unhealthy Ways of Coping 40

Restoratively Expressing Your Guilt, Shame, and Regret. . . .41

Unmasking Guilt 42

Mustering Courage. 43

The Needs of Mourning. 44

How to Talk about Your Guilt .47

Damaging Expression Versus Restorative Expression. . . .50

White Lies and Secrets. 52

The Gifts of Vulnerability. 53

Making Things Right 55

A Final Word 57

WELCOME

"Guilt is perhaps the most painful companion of death."
— Coco Chanel

If you're reading this book, you are probably feeling guilty, ashamed, or regretful in the aftermath of the death of someone loved or another significant life loss (or you're trying to help someone else who is).

The first thing I want to do is assure you that all your emotions are normal. While feelings of guilt, shame, and regret in grief are painful, they are common and natural. There is nothing wrong with you. In fact, guilty feelings can mean that you have a developed sense of right and wrong, that you care about others and your relationships with them, and that you strive to be a better person.

The second thing I want to do is promise you that you can find relief from these hurtful feelings. That's the purpose of this little book, in fact. When you become better acquainted with your guilt, shame, or regret, and work on understanding and restoratively expressing it, over time it will soften. It may seem counterintuitive to you right now, but the truth is that like all feelings in grief, your guilt is trying to teach you something. And if you allow it to speak—if you give it the time and attention it needs and deserves—it will lighten. It will no longer weigh so heavily on your heart and cause you so much pain.

The goal is to help you find a path through and beyond your feelings of guilt, shame, or regret. While in the short run guilt and its associated emotions are normal, they can become harmful to you. Feelings of guilt, shame, and regret are meant to be experienced and worked through—not lived in, day in and day out, forever.

Let's get started.

MY GUILT, SHAME, AND REGRET

Before we go any further, please take a moment to jot down a few notes about any guilty, shameful, or regretful feelings you've been experiencing so far in your grief journey.

Since the loss, I've been feeling _____

_____

_____

_____

_____

I think I've been feeling guilt, shame, or regret about the loss because _____

_____

_____

_____

_____

I'm reading this book to _____

_____

_____

_____

_____

_____

GUILT, SHAME, AND REGRET

Guilt, shame, and regret are close cousins. They belong to a group of feelings psychologists calls the "self-conscious emotions." This means that they are feelings of self-awareness. In other words, they're emotions we have about ourselves. The more positive self-conscious emotions include pride and self-confidence. Empathy, too, is a self-conscious emotion because it is mirroring, inside our own consciousness, the feelings we witness in others.

What do guilt, shame, and regret have in common?

JUDGMENT

It's important to note that the self-conscious emotions are self-evaluative. In other words, they arise when we are judging ourselves. What are we judging? We're measuring ourselves against the yardstick of our social and cultural rules and values. Human beings have many, many rules, expectations, and values, spoken and unspoken. When a child sneaks a cookie from the kitchen cabinet without permission, they may feel guilty because they know it's against their parents' rules and that breaking rules is bad. Or when we neglect to clean up after our dog or cut in a line, we may feel a twinge of guilt because we know we've done something that's broadly disapproved of and can have a negative effect on others. In other words, we've done something that falls short of our standards of morality. Think of the self-conscious emotions as the moral emotions.

Scientists who study human behavior now know that the self-conscious emotions typically first appear when children are about two to three years old. We start understanding social rules and values and judging our own behavior against them early on. After that, throughout our lives, most of us experience the self-conscious emotions countless times—as often as every day—in ways big and small. But now that you're in grief, as a consequence of a significant loss, you may be finding yourself struggling in a more profound and painful way with guilt, shame, and/or regret. If so, it's OK. We're going to talk openly and lovingly about these feelings and what to do with them. They're normal. You're normal.

BACKWARD-LOOKING

What's more, guilt, shame, and regret are backward-looking emotions. You feel them in the now, but they're caused by memories of things done (or not done) in the past.

One big lesson I've learned in my many years as a grief

counselor is that in grief, it's instinctive and necessary to go backward before we can go forward. When someone we love dies, we naturally turn around, toward remembering the time we shared with them. We reminisce. We think and talk about specific moments, incidents, days, and periods of time.

We do this in part to tell ourselves the story of the person's life and our relationship with them. As even a child knows, a story has a beginning, a middle, and an end. The end has now happened, so it's time to go back and connect all the parts and pieces and build a complete, coherent story that makes sense to us.

So, the backward-looking nature of guilt, shame, and regret in grief is normal and necessary. Whether your grief journey includes guilt or not, it's good to excavate the past, look at old photos and videos, share stories, and talk about what happened. In fact, remembering the past is what makes hoping for the future possible. The key is not to get stuck in the past, which is why befriending and integrating guilty feelings is so important. You won't be able to eventually move forward unless you do so.

SECRECY

Have you felt yourself concealing the guilt of your grief? Have you noticed that you would prefer to keep it a secret? Guilt, shame, and regret tend to live in the deep, dark corners. They often hide. They typically don't like to be revealed.

In grief psychology, we sometimes talk about disenfranchisement. Certain types of loss tend to be stigmatized, and the people grieving those deaths or losses often experience disenfranchised grief. This means that their grief is often not broadly acknowledged or well-supported by their community. Sometimes it's even shamed. Examples include grief following suicides, overdoses, murders, and deaths caused by mental-health crises.

We tend to stigmatize guilt, shame, and regret in similar ways. They're often based on secrets, and we keep them a secret because we feel ashamed. Then they become even more secret because we haven't brought them into the light in a timely fashion—at the time of the loss. So we feel even more ashamed and the downward spiral continues.

Secrecy is not your friend if you hope to heal in grief. All your feelings need to be acknowledged, encountered, and shared outside of yourself if they are to soften. They need the light of affirmation and the balm of normalization.

HEALING IN GRIEF

To heal in grief means to become whole again, to integrate your grief into your self and to find a path to continue your changed life with fullness and meaning. Your guilty feelings are part of your grief, and to heal them you will learn to understand them, befriend them, and express them in restorative ways. Through this process your guilt will soften, allowing you to move through and beyond the intensity with which you are experiencing it now.

GUILT, SHAME, OR REGRET?

So far we've been lumping the feelings of guilt, shame, and regret together. Now let's take a look at the differences among them. They're similar, but they're not the same. Understanding which you are feeling, to what degree, and why will help you get to know your grief, embrace and express it, and journey on.

Guilt

When we intentionally act against our own values or the values of those we respect, most of us naturally feel guilty. (People with narcissistic or sociopathic personalities are incapable of experiencing guilt, shame, and regret.) When you say, "If only I hadn't…," that's usually guilt talking. Guilt is the feeling that we've knowingly done something wrong, and if we get blamed or called out about it, we deserve it. We all make bad decisions and choices sometimes. It's human nature to experiment, learn, and, we hope, grow. (Also see the section on clean guilt versus dirty guilt on page 13.)

Guilt can be a constructive emotion. It focuses externally, on the impact we have on other people. Perhaps counterintuitively, it gives us a sense of control: I did this bad thing, so then this happened. We can see and "own" the cause and effect. When it is explored and expressed, guilt not only helps us navigate and adapt in life and relationships, it gives us the motivation and opportunity to take responsibility, seek forgiveness, and make things right when necessary. It can restore our feelings of self-pride and help bring us to healing.

Shame

Shame, sometimes called the toxic cousin of guilt, is a feeling of unworthiness. It tends to be a more deep-seated, long-term self-judgment. If you feel like something is inherently wrong with you, that's shame. If you think you're to blame for others' bad actions because you're defective or not good enough in some way, that's shame. As Brené Brown says, "The difference between shame and guilt is the difference between 'I am bad' and 'I did something bad.'"

Shame is a destructive, disabling emotion. It focuses internally. It's based on an inaccurate understanding of innate self-worth. Doing something bad is not the same as *being* bad.

Shame is often (but not always) the result of abuse of some kind (physical, sexual, emotional, psychological, cultural).

The Guilt of Grief

Over time, it tends to cripple lives and can lead to mental-health challenges such as clinical depression and substance-use disorder.

If you think shame might be part of your grief experience or overall life struggles, I encourage you to make an appointment with a compassionate grief counselor. Getting to the bottom of shame is often difficult, and you need and deserve professional support as you do this critical work. The good news is that exploring and healing shame can transform your life. As you learn about the origins of your shame and bring what has been hidden in darkness into the cleansing light of day, your self-esteem will become stronger and your experience of life more satisfying and joyful.

Regret

Regret is what we feel when we make a choice that, unbeknownst to us at the time, will later cause us pain or harm. When you say, "I wish that I had…," that's regret speaking. Regret often has to do with feelings of missed opportunity or lack of control or foresight. It's a "hindsight-is-20/20" emotion.

For example, let's say we miss a family reunion because we have an important work commitment on the same day. Choosing to follow through with the work commitment could be a perfectly logical, reasonable, and even necessary choice at the time. It's consistent with our own rules and values. (Keep the job! Pay the mortgage! Take care of the family!) But if a beloved cousin attends the reunion then unexpectedly dies the next week, we're likely to regret having missed that precious, final opportunity to spend time with them.

Regret can make us feel more helpless than guilt because it emphasizes our lack of control in life. We live in a world in which we make countless choices every day, and we can't accurately predict the consequences of every single choice. Taking one route to get to a destination versus another might seem like a coin toss at the time, but if the course we choose happens to put us in the path of an oncoming drunk driver, we will probably later experience regret (among other feelings), even though we did nothing wrong.

Guilt, shame, and regret can overlap, of course. They're often not so neatly separated in real life. What's more, you may feel all three of these feelings to different degrees and for different reasons—at different times or at the same time! Still, I hope this discussion helped you understand your particular feelings a bit better. From here forward in this book, I'm generally going to use the word "guilt" to mean any or all of the three feelings. When you read "guilt," please feel free to substitute the self-conscious emotion(s) you're feeling most strongly or having the most trouble with at the time.

CLEAN GUILT VERSUS DIRTY GUILT

"Clean pain" is the normal pain that follows difficult life experiences. "Dirty pain" is the damaging, multiplied pain we create when we catastrophize, judge ourselves unfairly, or allow ourselves to be judged by others. Is the guilt you're feeling clean or dirty?

I once companioned a grieving middle-aged woman who suffered from terrible guilt after her elderly mother died. The woman had a full life, including a job, a husband, and three children at home. Her mother, whose health was slowly declining, lived several states away. The woman visited her mother a couple of times a year, but her life obligations were such that she could not be with her mother often, and when the mother died, the woman could not shake the feeling that she was a bad person. Her grief was marked by pronounced self-blame and self-punishment. She was experiencing dirty guilt.

I created a safe space in which this woman could express her feelings of guilt. Over time, I also helped her come to the understanding that her mother knew she loved her dearly. What's more, when she was able to spend time with her mother, she took good care of her. She did everything she could given the many necessary obligations of her life.

With dirty guilt, you are telling yourself a story about

how you should have been able to avoid or control an unavoidable, uncontrollable situation (and others may be trying to blame you by telling you that story as well). Or your guilt is regret, which sees with hindsight and tries to accept more blame than is justified.

Clean guilt, on the other hand, is what you may feel after you make an actual mistake or error in judgment. In this case, your feelings of guilt are justified and natural. They are clean.

NOTE: if your accidental or intentional actions directly contributed to a death or another significant loss, please seek help from an experienced, well-trained grief counselor. Your feelings of guilt and remorse will certainly complicate your grief journey, and you will probably need professional assistance effectively engaging with and working through them. Depending on the loss, you may even be suffering from post-traumatic grief or PTSD. Please, do right by yourself and those who care about you and get the help you need.

Both clean and dirty guilt are normal, valid feelings. But dirty guilt is typically the result of unrealistic, unreasonable, or illogical expectations. If others are saying things to you like "It wasn't your fault" or "There's no way you could have…," you may be experiencing dirty guilt. If this is happening to you, try thinking of your guilty feelings as regrets, instead, and see if that helps you better encounter them.

Whether your guilt is clean or dirty, however, it's necessary to understand, explore, and restoratively express it in order to find your way back to hope and healing.

TYPES OF GUILT

In addition to the distinction between clean guilt and dirty guilt, there are several common types of guilt that I have often borne witness to in my four decades as a grief counselor.

Survivor guilt

Sometimes being alive after someone you love has died causes what's termed "survivor guilt." For example, in the aftermath of 9/11, I counseled several people who worked in the World Trade Center and made it out alive, though their coworkers did not. They struggled with survivor guilt. Have you found yourself thinking, "Why did someone I care about die and not me?" or "I wish it had been me instead"? These are normal thoughts, and they may be part of your grief experience.

Relief guilt

If someone you love dies after a long period of illness and suffering, you may naturally feel some relief. But your feelings of relief can also make you feel guilty. "I shouldn't be feeling relieved," you might think. Relief-guilt may also arise when you recognize that you won't miss certain aspects of the relationship you had with a person who died. For example, you probably wouldn't miss being belittled or any behavior that caused family distress. Or, to give a milder example, you likely wouldn't miss being late to appointments because the person who died was always running behind schedule. To not miss some things or to be glad that difficult times are over doesn't mean you didn't love the person, however. It's perfectly normal to feel both relief and deep sadness at the same time.

Joy-guilt

Like relief-guilt, joy-guilt is about thinking that lighter, happier feelings are wrong at a time of loss. Experiencing any kind of joy after a death can make you feel guilty. One day you might find yourself smiling or laughing at something, only to chastise yourself for having felt happy for a minute. It's as if your loyalty to the person who died demands that you be sad all the time now that they're gone. That's not true, of course. As you do the work of mourning, your natural healing journey will allow to start experiencing more and more levity and less and less pain.

Magical thinking and guilt

Consciously or unconsciously wishing for the death of someone loved—and then having that "wish" come true— can make you feel guilty. We call this magical thinking,

The Guilt of Grief

because, of course, your thoughts did not cause the death. At some point in your relationship, you may have thought or even said aloud, "I wish you would go away and leave me alone." Or, if the relationship was extremely difficult, you might have had more direct thoughts about death ending the relationship. If so, you may now feel somehow responsible for the death. Know that all relationships have moments in which negative, irrational thoughts prevail. But even so, your mind doesn't have the power to inflict death.

Longstanding personality factors

Some people have felt guilty their entire lives. I hope you're not one of them, but you may be. Why? Because some people are taught early in life, typically during childhood, that they are responsible when something bad happens. When someone dies, it's just one more thing to feel guilty about. If all-encompassing guilt or shame is part of your experience, please seek out a professional counselor who can help you work on understanding your feelings of self-worth and rebuilding your self-esteem. You are a precious, one-of-a-kind human being.

UNDERSTANDING YOUR GUILT

"Guilt isn't always a rational thing...Guilt is a weight that will crush you whether you deserve it or not."
— Maureen Johnson

Getting to the bottom of your guilty feelings is a process that will take time and dedication. I know it may not be easy, because exploring feelings of guilt requires revisiting things we believe we did wrong or are wrong with us. That is painful work. But I also know it's worth it. These feelings are probably absorbing a lot of your psychic energy right now, anyway. The choice you have before you is to continue to be drained by them, living in the numbness of denial or the pain of self-recrimination, or to explore them openly and engage with them productively. The latter is both a wise and self-compassionate choice. This book will help guide you.

THE WOLFELT GUILT INVENTORY
Now let's take a minute to learn more about your particular experiences with guilt, both in relation to your loss and more generally, to see how guilty self-conscious feelings may have been part of your life story and personality.

I've created the following questionnaire to help you take a closer look at your guilt and begin to identify areas of focus for restoratively expressing and reconciling it. Next to each statement, please circle the number that fits best. As you read each question, please consider not only guilt but shame and regret as well.

THE WOLFELT GUILT INVENTORY Next to each statement, circle the number that fits best.	Never	Rarely	Sometimes	Often
In the household I grew up in, people were made to feel guilty. Guilt was wielded as a form of control.	1	2	3	4
As a child and young person, I believe I felt guilt or shame more than my friends and peers.	1	2	3	4
As a child and young person, the adults in my life modeled unhealthy guilt/shame or tried to make others feel guilty/ashamed in unhealthy ways.	1	2	3	4
I have suffered abuse (physical, sexual, emotional, psychological, and/or cultural).	1	2	3	4
FAMILY OF ORIGIN SCORE (out of 16)				
In the past, there have been times I have felt guilty about a life loss but didn't express it.	1	2	3	4
I still feel unreconciled guilt or shame about things that happened earlier in my life.	1	2	3	4

Guilt or shame has been a prominent part of my life.	1	2	3	4

CARRIED GRIEF SCORE (out of 12)

I feel generalized guilt and can't always identify why.	1	2	3	4
I feel guilty about this loss.	1	2	3	4
I feel guilty but don't express my guilt fully.	1	2	3	4
When I'm feeling guilty lately, I tend to withdraw and isolate.	1	2	3	4
I'm afraid of fully exploring and expressing my guilt.	1	2	3	4

INTERNAL GUILT SCORE (out of 20)

I do things to try to make up for what I feel guilty about instead of fully exploring my guilt.	1	2	3	4
Others say I shouldn't feel so guilty.	1	2	3	4
I'm afraid my guilt or shame is harming others in my family.	1	2	3	4
People comment on my low self-esteem.	1	2	3	4

EXTERNAL GUILT SCORE (out of 16)

I wish I didn't feel so guilty or ashamed.	1	2	3	4
I need to better acknowledge and understand my guilt.	1	2	3	4
I need to develop healthier ways of expressing my guilt.	1	2	3	4
My guilt is blocking healing, peace, love, and joy.	1	2	3	4

GUILT AWARENESS SCORE (out of 16)

TOTAL SCORE (out of 80)

Before we talk about guilt scores, I want to emphasize that guilt is not truly a measurable experience. The scale I've created is meant only to help you begin to understand your guilt better. With that caveat firmly in mind, I invite you to use this rubric to get a sense of the extent of your guilt issues.

0-25	Minimal guilt
26-40	Mild guilt
41-60	Moderate guilt
61-80	Severe guilt

In addition to helping you understand the severity of your guilt, the labeled sections in the chart will also give you some hints about where to concentrate your energies as you work on reconciling your guilt. If your internal guilt score is high but your external guilt score is low, for example, you may not be expressing your feelings of guilt nearly enough. If your family of origin and carried grief scores are high, you may need the support of a counselor in understanding how your early experiences with guilt, shame, and/or abuse are shaping your current struggles—and what to do about that. And since awareness is the first step toward positive change, your guilt awareness score measures how conscious you are of any significant guilt issues and your readiness to work on them.

CONTRIBUTORS TO GUILT IN GRIEF

Following are the most common contributors to guilt in grief. As you read through them, put a checkmark next to any that might apply to you.

☐ *Circumstances of the loss*

Understandably, this is often a major contributor to feelings of guilt after a loss. Remember that feelings of right and wrong about one's own behavior are often at the heart of guilt. Do you feel you did something wrong that somehow contributed to the death or loss? Do you feel you didn't do something that you should have?

Earlier we discussed stigmatized losses and disenfranchised grief. Was the death or loss stigmatized in any way? Is it a type of loss that people tend to judge unfairly? If so, this is probably causing or adding to your feelings of guilt or shame.

In addition, you may be feeling guilty about circumstances or events before or after the loss. Did something happen in the days, weeks, or years leading up to the loss that you feel guilty about? Or do you feel bad about something that happened after the loss—maybe something you said or a way in which you behaved? This, too, is a common influence on the experience of guilt in the aftermath of a loss.

Stop and take a moment to tell more of the story of your loss and why you feel guilty about it:

_____

_____

_____

_____

_____

_____

☐ *Your relationship with the person/people you associate with your guilt*

Unexpected deaths often result in feelings of unfinished business. Regardless of who is "at fault," you may feel guilty about any longstanding or unreconciled relationship issues. It's so hard to be forever robbed of the opportunity to clear the air and make things right.

If your feelings of guilt are directed at people who are still alive, on the other hand, the unique features of your relationships and history with them will also affect your grief. The good news is that it's not too late in this case to clear the air and make things right.

☐ *Family-of-origin experience*

When you were growing up, how were guilt and shame modeled in your home? Were you made to feel guilty often? How and why? Did your family harbor shame about something? Did your parents or others make you feel ashamed?

In general, were feelings accepted and openly discussed in your family, or were feelings considered private and not to be expressed or discussed? Did members of your family support one another emotionally? Was love unconditional or conditional?

We learn so much about how to "be" from our parents and other adult caregivers. You may have been taught that it's normal or even good to feel guilty. In some family traditions, guilt is the main method of control, and if your guilt keeps your behavior in check, you're rewarded for that.

Your guilt style was affected by your upbringing. You may be repeating patterns you learned at home, or you may have chosen, consciously or unconsciously, to do the opposite. Whatever your go-to guilt script is, it is probably now coming to the fore in your grief. What was your "Family of Origin Score" on page 20? A high score indicates that you may have deep-seated guilt or shame habits to learn more about.

☐ *Personality factors*
Some of us are introverts, and some are extroverts. Some are risk-takers, and others are cautious. Some engage with their

hearts, and some lead with their minds. Some are doers, and some are observers. Independent of your upbringing at home, you have grown into a unique individual shaped by all kinds of people, life experiences, cultural influences, and genetics. Your guilt response in grief will be influenced by all of it.

In addition, your self-esteem plays a role in your guilt response. Remember how we said that guilt is self-judgment? When faced with a major loss, people who tend to judge themselves severely may more naturally struggle with guilt. After all, they may think, I am not a good/strong/kind/ worthy person, so I surely deserve some blame for this loss. People with stronger self-esteem, on the other hand, might make others feel guilty or ashamed as an unhealthy way of coping with their grief.

☐ *Carried grief*

Obviously, life is a series of losses and transitions. It is likely that your life experiences to date include significant losses other than the loss that is arousing your guilt right now. If so, you may be carrying old grief that is contributing to your current feelings of guilt. Unreconciled issues from our past often affect our ongoing lives in ways we don't fully appreciate or understand.

Over the years, guilty feelings can really snowball. Take a

look at your "Carried Grief Score" on page 21. If it's 9 or higher, you may essentially be rolling old guilt or shame into your current guilty feelings without realizing it.

☐ *Your current life circumstances and relationships*
How was your life going before this loss? If you were already struggling—with relationships, family, career, health, finances, or other major stressors—the loss may feel like the straw that broke the camel's back. Regrets may be weighing on you for many reasons. Alternately, your life may have been going along just fine, but you now realize you lack the intimate relationships you need for adequate emotional and social support. Feelings of guilt and shame can interfere with establishing and maintaining strong relationships.

☐ *Your spirituality*
Do religious and spiritual background and beliefs influence guilt? Absolutely! We've all heard of Catholic guilt. However, in reality, guilt is not exclusive to Catholics or any other one religion. Religious rules and understandings sometimes contribute to generalized guilt and shame.

If you were raised in the Christian, Jewish, or Muslim faith, maybe you were taught that you harbor original sin, continue to sin often, and are obligated to frequently repent and ask for forgiveness. Or maybe you learned that God is always judging you. Or perhaps you came to understand that mere thoughts of ill will, selfishness, or vanity are proof that you (and all people) are inherently bad. In Far Eastern spiritual traditions, on the other hand, guilt is sometimes considered unnecessary or stunting. Either way, as you become better acquainted with your guilt, consider how your spiritual beliefs may be part of the mix.

☐ *Cultural expectations*

The expectations or mores of the culture you belong to can also influence your feelings of guilt in grief. For example, what are your community's rules, spoken or unspoken, about what you should/shouldn't do or how you should/ shouldn't behave after a loss? If you've violated or neglected any of these rules, you may feel guilty about it. Your role within your community may also affect what's considered appropriate behavior for you. If you're a young person, for instance, maybe you're supposed to treat your elders in a certain way. Or perhaps gender expectations in your culture have had a bearing on your guilt.

These aren't all the contributors to guilt in grief, of course, but they're the ones I've seen most in my forty years counseling people in grief. As you read this section, did you think of other influences on your feelings of guilt or shame since the loss? Write them down here:

The Guilt of Grief

Possible contributors to my guilt in grief:

_____

_____

_____

TO ERR IS HUMAN

They say that the only two sure things in life are death and taxes. To that I would like to add mistakes.

To be human is to be imperfect. We're born knowing almost nothing save instinctual responses, and from there we learn by seeing and doing. In fact, our entire lives are learning experiences.

From our parents and our communities, we learn right from wrong. We also learn how to deal with inevitable mistakes. Do we treat them as normal course corrections that help us do better next time? Or do we consider them failures that we should be ashamed of?

If you're prone to guilt or shame in general, it's likely because you were taught the latter. But the truth is that it's normal to make mistakes. Actually, making lots of mistakes can mean you're fully engaging with life and trying many new things.

You can choose to cultivate a growth mindset from here forward. That means that when mistakes come along, as they will, you're eager to learn from them and do better next time. You set down guilt and shame, and you work on resiliency, perseverance, and self-love. You're perfectly imperfect.

THE UTILITY OF GUILT

The fact that guilt exists is all the reason we need to accept it as a normal part of human life. All emotions are natural, and this includes the self-conscious emotions of guilt, shame, and regret.

But as I mentioned earlier, feelings of morality also serve a purpose in our lives. They encourage us to act responsibly. In fact, they help us understand what responsible behavior is. They direct us to consider others. They remind us that we are part of a community that needs rules and mutual consideration to function. They're the guardrails that help keep society safe, vulnerable individuals protected, and families safeguarded. And they nurture one of the most meaningful emotions available to humankind: empathy.

Can you imagine a world with no morality? It's not a pretty picture, is it. Images from *Mad Max* and *A Clockwork Orange* spring to my mind. But as with everything in life, moderation is key. Not enough guilt and you have anarchy. Too much guilt and you have repression and misery. Let's talk about the dangers of guilt next.

THE DANGERS OF GUILT

Prolonged, pronounced guilt, shame, and regret are harmful to your wellbeing. As I said earlier, they're emotions that are meant to be experienced and worked through—not inhabited forever. Let's discuss the potential dangers of long-term, unreconciled guilt to your physical, emotional, social, and spiritual health.

Sustained, pronounced guilt stresses the body and causes illness. Shame, especially, can boost stress hormones that lead to inflammation and damage the immune system. It can contribute to depression and prevent happiness and joy.

Physical
What does guilt feel like in your body? Stop reading for a moment and see if you can locate the sensation and describe it to yourself. Where do you notice it? What are the qualities of the feeling?

Guilt often feels similar to how fear or worry feel in the body. This is because guilt releases the same stress hormone—cortisol—that anxiety does. Over time, too much cortisol in the body can lead to high blood pressure, higher risk of heart disease and diabetes, and clinical depression and anxiety disorders. What's more, research demonstrates that high guilt levels dampen the immune system. This makes people more vulnerable to illnesses and disease.

Guilt may also feel heavy, like a weight on your chest or an anchor dragging you down. In fact, studies have shown that the psychic burden of guilt makes physical tasks seem more difficult. Like depression, guilt can sap us of energy and drain our capacity to get things done.

Emotional

Guilt feels bad emotionally. That's probably why you've picked up this book. It hurts. Anything that hurts is a symptom that needs attention.

Social

Feelings of guilt, shame, and regret may well be negatively affecting your relationships. These emotions can lower your self-esteem, making you feel unsure of yourself and less worthy of love and care. You might avoid spending time with people. The secrecy of guilt may also make you feel unable to open up when you're around others for fear of disclosing something you're embarrassed about or feel ashamed of.

Think of guilt as a wall you're building around your heart, knowingly or unknowingly. It's likely blocking affection and companionship. It's getting in the way of close relationships. It's time to dismantle the wall, brick by brick.

Spiritual

Guilt shuts you down and can make you feel isolated, anxious, and burdened. Good spiritual health feels the opposite—light, curious, open, loving, and free. However, life's spiritual journey also includes encountering and wrestling with spiritual challenges as they arise, and the guilt of grief is one such challenge. So don't be afraid to draw upon, question, or confront your spiritual beliefs as you work to understand and restoratively express your guilt. Just remember that in the long term, ongoing, unrelenting guilt will get in the way of spiritual experiences like awe, gratitude, and joy.

Complicated Grief and Guilt

Ongoing, unrelenting guilt, shame, or regret is often a symptom of what many therapists term "complicated grief." But it's my belief that complicated grief isn't a disorder or illness; it's simply normal grief that has gotten stuck or off-track somehow, usually due to complicated loss or life circumstances.

I call grief that's stuck on a strong feeling such as guilt "impasse grief" because the guilt is creating an impasse to healing. It's like a giant boulder blocking a narrow mountain trail. You can't go around it. You can't go under it. You can't get over it. So every day you suffer guilt about the rock, and you go nowhere.

Is your guilt the main or most pronounced feeling in your grief? Do you feel generalized guilt, shame, or regret? Have you been feeling your guilt strongly for many months or years now—without it diminishing (and maybe even with it growing) over time? If you've answered yes to these questions, you're probably experiencing some natural complications of your grief. I hope this book will help you understand, embrace, and express your guilt so that it begins to soften. I also encourage you to make an appointment with a compassionate counselor. Seeing an experienced grief counselor for a period of weeks or months may be just the extra help you need to roll the boulder aside and find a way through this impasse to hope and healing.

BEFRIENDING YOUR GUILT, SHAME, AND REGRET

"Guilt, regret, resentment…and all forms of non-forgiveness are caused by too much past and not enough presence."
— Eckhart Tolle

Your feelings of guilt, shame, and regret are not your enemy. Yes, they are causing you pain, but they are there for a reason. They are there to teach you about your past, your ingrained thoughts and behaviors, and your choices moving forward. If we never felt guilt, shame, or regret, we would never see our mistakes or learn how to make better decisions next time.

To befriend your feelings is to be present to them. It is to turn toward them instead of away from them. It is to spend quality time with them instead of hiding from them. It is to bear witness to them and honor them. Consider that your grief—including your guilt—is your love in a different form. Regard it with compassion and tenderness, just as you do your love.

SAFETY FIRST

Guilt, shame, and regret cause anxiety, and anxiety makes us feel restless and unsafe. So when you're ready to spend time befriending your guilt, I want you to be sure to establish a sense of safety first.

Go somewhere you feel safe and calm. It might be your bedroom, your car, a forest trail, a friend's home—anywhere that you can focus on your emotions, express them however you want to without judgment, and feel that you'll be OK doing so. Have your pet or a close friend at your side if that enhances your feeling of safety. Create an even more comforting ambiance if you would like, with items such as a blanket, pillow, tissues, music, candles, aromatherapy, etc. If you have a linking object that reminds you of the person who died or the loss, especially if it helps you feel the love you have for them, hold it in your lap. And banish anything from your safety zone that makes you feel anxious.

If you don't feel safe, you won't be able to take the next step. So, safety first!

ONE DOSE AT A TIME

Grief is a lifetime experience. A significant loss often takes years to fully integrate into your heart and ongoing life. So, I urge you to take it not only one day at a time but one *dose* at a time. What do I mean by "dose"? A dose of grief is a brief, intentional encounter with your thoughts and feelings.

When a loss is fresh, your grief naturally pervades your days. It takes over. But in the weeks to follow, as life goes on, your grief begins to sit a little more quietly beside you. It's still there. It's still painful. But it no longer commands every moment of your attention.

Intermittently, however, your ongoing grief will prod you. You may feel a sharp pang out of nowhere. Or you may see a reminder and experience a burst of deep sorrow. Or you may be talking with someone, and your eyes will well with tears when the loss comes up. Or you may be lying in bed, unable to sleep, and your grief will again feel newly overwhelming. If guilt is a prominent part of your grief experience, your feelings of guilt may dominate these encounters, but they probably include many different thoughts and feelings.

In such moments, when your grief naturally comes to the fore, this is a dose of grief. Befriending your grief means accepting it in doses as it comes to you and when possible, stopping what you're doing and embracing it with acceptance and intention.

THE INTENTION OF BEFRIENDING

Unless we're in complete denial, we don't have to make an effort to grieve. Our grief naturally shows up after a significant loss. But to befriend our grief requires that we consciously make space for it—even welcome it into our lives.

Being intentional with your grief in this way means seeing it as the necessary and productive process it is. It also means learning more about healthy grieving (which you're doing by reading this book), taking daily steps that will help you heal, and fostering hope for your ongoing life.

Befriending Your Guilt, Shame, and Regret

Stop and take a moment to consider your intention for understanding, befriending, and restoratively expressing the guilt you've been experiencing in your grief. What is the best possible outcome you envision? Write it down here.

My Grief Intention _____

_____

_____

THE MINDFULNESS OF BEFRIENDING

Befriending grief also requires being aware of what you are feeling and mindfully engaging with those feelings.

Especially with deeply painful emotions such as guilt, it's easy to get caught in a cycle of fear and despair. In fact, you may be reluctant to befriend your guilty feelings because you're afraid that digging too deeply will only make you feel worse.

When you feel like you may be wallowing too much or slipping into hopelessness, look back at your intention and consider ways you could try engaging with your guilt more mindfully. You're still going to allow and accept these feelings, but you're also going to *do something* different with them. Try observing them as a therapist might and give yourself some compassionate advice. Talk to yourself with self-love and forgiveness. Turn to mindfulness practices such as meditation, yoga, and spending time in nature. And rely on the "Restoratively Expressing" section of this book, beginning on page 41.

The Guilt of Grief

Remember, hopelessness and despair are not mindful. If you're overly disheartened, you're probably not intentionally and mindfully befriending...instead, you're stuck. Ask for help getting unstuck, and work through the guidance in this book.

BEFRIENDING YOUR GUILT

The next time you're feeling your grief-related guilt, plan to spend a few minutes with it.

1. Retreat to your safe space and sit still. Breathe in and out, deeply and slowly. Close your eyes if this helps you concentrate.

2. Now notice what your guilt feels like in your body. Describe it silently or, if you want to, out loud. "My chest feels tight," you might say, "and my eyes are burning like I might cry." Cry if you feel like crying. Continue to simply observe the feeling in your body for a minute or so. Keep breathing deeply.

3. Next, give your feeling a name and, if you can, the reason(s) behind it. Say it silently or, if you want to, out loud. "I'm feeling so much regret that I had a chance to see him, and I didn't take it," you might say. If your guilt has to do with a death, you can also try directing your thoughts at the person who died: "I'm feeling so much regret that I had a chance to see you, but I didn't take it..." Or you can turn your talk into a prayer if that works for you. For a minute or two, keep exploring your feeling in words, spoken or unspoken, as you continue to breathe deeply.

4. Next, pivot to pondering the love or attachment you continue to feel for the person who died or the thing that you lost. Feel that love in your body, and express it in words if you would like. Do this for a minute or two.

5. Finally, turn that love back on yourself. Close with a mantra that emphasizes self-acceptance and -love. You might try something like "My grief is normal and necessary. I am learning to understand and embrace my grief. I am a work in progress." Repeat for a minute or so.

6. Open your eyes, stand, and stretch. Do you feel differently than you did before you intentionally engaged with the guilt of your grief?

UNHEALTHY WAYS OF COPING

I know that your guilt is painful, and when we're in pain, it's natural to seek relief from that pain. Some forms of emotional pain relief are healthy, such as expressing your feelings, physical activity, prayer/meditation, and fun (but temporary and safe) distraction. But other common pain-relief methods are not healthy. These include overuse of drugs or alcohol, other addictive behaviors (shopping, gambling, sex), and self-harm. Not only can unhealthy coping mechanisms hurt your body, your relationships, and your financial wellbeing, they do not help you integrate your grief and heal. In fact, they will only make your complicated grief more complicated.

RESTORATIVELY EXPRESSING YOUR GUILT, SHAME, AND REGRET

"There are two kinds of guilt: the kind that drowns you until you're useless, and the kind that fires your soul to purpose."
— Sabaa Tahir

Your grief is all the thoughts and emotions you have inside you about the loss. Grieving is feeling your loss on the inside. Mourning, on the other hand, is expressing your grief on the outside. Mourning is giving voice to your grief and sharing it with others. Mourning is what gives your grief momentum. Mourning is how you heal.

In this section we'll talk about why it's essential to not just grieve but actively mourn your guilt. We'll look at the difference between potentially damaging expressions of guilt and restorative expressions of guilt. And we'll consider the role of forgiveness and making amends.

UNMASKING GUILT

It's time to revisit the inherently secretive nature of guilt.

Befriending your guilt is an individual, internal process. You may think that getting to know your guilt, allowing and accepting it, and experiencing it inside of you with intention and mindfulness is enough—even if it's still a secret. It's not. You also need to express your guilt outside of yourself. You need to share it with others. This means, of course, breaking through any secretive feelings you may have about your guilt.

Why do you need to share your guilt with others? Two reasons. First, all grief feelings must be expressed, or mourned, to be worked through and healed. No exceptions. And second, guilt in particular requires social review and affirmation because, as we've said, it is based on self-judgment about social rules. The only way to fully bear witness to your guilt is to have it heard and considered by members of your community. If you never share your guilt outside of yourself, you will always carry that feeling of secrecy and, likely, shame.

No matter what you are feeling guilty, ashamed, or regretful about, it's necessary to talk to family members and/or friends about it. Remember that guilt is a very normal, understandable human experience. Rest assured that most of the time, feelings of guilt are associated with behaviors or decisions that those who care about you will readily empathize with. We have all made mistakes. We all experience guilt and regret. We understand.

And even in situations in which the grieving person did something wrong or even unconscionable, the only way to begin to work through the issue, make amends, restore peace of mind, and live fully again is to tell the truth about what happened as well as the thoughts and feelings that accompany it.

Unmasking guilt makes most grievers feel deeply relieved. If you're fearful of sharing your guilty feelings outside of yourself, remember that it's OK to take it one tiny step at a time.

MUSTERING COURAGE

Everyone grieves, but it takes courage to mourn, especially when it comes to feelings of guilt, shame, and regret. It's hard to admit guilt. To open up and lay ourselves bare. To expose our most tender inner secrets and feelings of wrongdoing so they can be judged by others.

In grief, as in most things, bravery begets more bravery. We find that if we muster the courage, finally, to tell a friend a hard truth about our grief, we have more courage for the next mourning opportunity. That's because usually our courage is rewarded. We put ourselves out there, and in doing so we notice that others offer empathy and support. We also feel a sense of relief and release just from having unburdened ourselves for the moment. In grief, bravery can foster healing.

THE NEEDS OF MOURNING

Your guilt is a symptom of your grief. As we've said, to reconcile your grief requires expressing it outside of yourself, or mourning it. In your journey through mourning, you must meet six needs along the way to healing.

THE SIX NEEDS OF MOURNING

1. Acknowledge the reality of the loss
2. Embrace the pain
3. Remember the person or attachment
4. Develop a new self-identity
5. Search for meaning
6. Let others help you—now and always

While a full discussion of the six needs of mourning is beyond the scope of this resource, here I want to highlight a few of the needs that have particular relevance to the expression of guilt. (For more on the six needs, please see my book *Understanding Your Grief*.)

The first need of mourning is to **acknowledge the reality of the loss**. Does the guilt you are experiencing have anything to do with the circumstances of the loss? If so, learning more about what happened and discussing your feelings of guilt associated with the circumstances with others will help you better acknowledge this difficult reality. Anything that helps you understand and comes to terms with the facts of the loss is a step in the right direction. For example, if you have lingering questions or potentially inaccurate assumptions about what happened, learn more. Muster the courage to ask questions, talk to those with additional information, gather many perspectives, and flesh out the story. Don't look away—look toward. You may learn that your fears or assumptions are unfounded. Or you might discover that there is more to the story than you realized. I know this process can be quite painful, but my hope is it will help you clarify the reality of the circumstances of the loss and better come to terms with the truth of your own potential culpability, if any. Your conversations with others as you undertake this research will often result in them sharing their normal guilty feelings, as well.

More generally, openness and honesty will give you momentum in moving through your guilt. Telling the story of the loss will help you more deeply acknowledge its reality, so that you come to understand it not only with your head, but with your heart. Talk about the loss. Tell others what happened. Include all the parts of the timeline of the story: the prologue, the beginning, the middle, the climax, the ending, and the epilogue.

Doing memory work—the third need of mourning—will also help you better understand your guilt and place it in the context of the entire relationship. Spend time looking at old photos and memorabilia. Put together a box of special snapshots and keepsakes. Share memories with others. Write down memories in a journal. The more you purposefully remember a variety of moments—not only but including those you feel some guilt about—the more likely you are to begin to realize that the past is a patchwork of both good and bad, love and strife. This is often true for many of us.

And finally, set aside time to work on the **fifth need of mourning—search for meaning**. These are activities in which you contemplate your biggest questions about the meaning of life and death. Taking part in spiritual services or rituals, writing down philosophical thoughts in a journal, and spending time in nature are three common ways people get in touch with their spirits. Your guilt is likely focused on snapshots in time. The search for meaning, conversely, ponders much longer spans—decades, lifetimes, millennia.

In addition to considering the meaning of the relationship and the loss in your life so far, you will also begin to look ahead as you search for meaning. What is the big picture for you? How do you find meaning in life? How could you spend your time in the years to come to ensure they're the most fulfilling? Rediscovering meaning in life is largely

The Guilt of Grief

a forward-looking project, while your guilt is backward-looking. Both are necessary, and at first it's appropriate for you to spend time looking back at and exploring whatever it is you feel guilty about. But over time, you will need more forward momentum to carry you into your future.

HOW TO TALK ABOUT YOUR GUILT

There are really no hard and fast rules about talking about your guilt and sharing any secrets you may be harboring. Do take a look at the section on page 50 about damaging expression vs. restorative expression. And in general, keep reminding yourself that talking about your feelings is healthy and, over time, healing.

Choosing listeners

As we've reviewed, guilty feelings arise from self-judgment. We feel guilty when we think we've done something wrong. When you're considering who to share your guilty thoughts and feelings with, choose those with the strongest empathy and the least tendency for judgment. They will be your best sounding boards and helpers.

Depending on the circumstances associated with your feelings of guilt, shame, and regret, you may already feel comfortable talking about them. If so, I would simply encourage you to continue to share them openly with others as they arise. If you're concerned that your friends and family are becoming fatigued with your expressions of guilt, consider joining a grief support group and/or seeing a grief counselor.

Starting with an outsider
If you're worried that sharing your guilt with certain people you care about may hurt them in some way or damage your relationship, start instead by talking about your guilt with a more objective outsider. This could be a counselor, or it could be a friend who's a good listener and cares about you but doesn't have a vested, personal interest in this particular loss.

Not only will sharing your guilty feelings with an outsider give you good practice in expressing them, this person can help you work through the sometimes tricky decisions about the whos, whats, and hows of sharing your guilt with those more intimately involved.

If you're reticent about talking about your guilty feelings and the circumstances that are making you feel guilty, start small. Tell one person one tiny thing and see what happens. Build from there. Keep the momentum going by opening up more and more. Don't share one time and then stop. If your guilt is still bothering you, that means you need to continue sharing.

Asking others to listen without premature dismissal
Your most important task in mourning your guilt is to share what you're thinking and feeling. Tell the story to people you

know to be good listeners. Even good listeners, though, are sometimes challenged by the self-judgments of others. You'll find that empathetic people often want to quickly dismiss any feelings of guilt. "You didn't do anything wrong," they may jump in and say almost right way. "I don't think you should give that a second thought."

It can feel affirming to be so easily cleared of any wrongdoing, but dismissing guilt too readily is just like dismissing any other grief feeling too readily. If you were instead told, "You shouldn't be so sad"—that would be grief-denying, right? Well so is discounting feelings of guilt. It's OK to ask your listeners to fully hear you out. What you're hoping for is the opportunity to share all of your guilty thoughts and feelings, and those may be tangled up with other grief thoughts and feeling as well. Exploring all of it thoroughly is essential for you, and over the course of the coming weeks and months, you might need to talk about it many times. Being cut off prematurely in your exploration will only keep you at an impasse. When you're ready, it's also OK to ask for advice. Just understand that receiving advice and potentially being told you did nothing wrong will likely not dispatch with your guilt once and for all. Instead, healing guilt is generally more of a dosed experience (see page 36) that will require multiple encounters.

Owning your guilt

The outside world may or may not consider your guilt "justified." It doesn't really matter (though do see the special note on page 14). If you're feeling guilt, that means it's a normal part of your grief journey and you need to talk about it. As you're talking about it, try to distinguish between being "at fault" for a wrongdoing and experiencing guilt. Own the latter. You are experiencing guilt and you need to talk about. Your feelings of guilt are real. Try not to blame or shame others for your guilt. Instead, if others are contributing to your feelings of guilt, explain how by using "I" statements. For example, "I feel guilty because I love my mother and wish I'd been with her when she fell" owns the root of your guilty feelings more than "I feel guilty because my sister is blaming me." Your sister may be blaming you, but your guilty feelings are yours, not hers. What is their true source? Think and talk this through.

DAMAGING EXPRESSION VERSUS RESTORATIVE EXPRESSION

To move toward reconciling your grief, you absolutely need to express your guilty feelings. There is no healing without mourning. But as you explore ways to befriend and express your guilt, I want you to keep in mind the difference between damaging expression and restorative expression.

Damaging expression of guilty feelings harms you or others. It hurts feelings and injures relationships. If your loss experience was traumatic, it can even cause secondary trauma to others who may not be trained or equipped to make space for and process the traumas of others.

Restorative expression of guilt, on the other hand, allows you to fully share feelings in ways and places that are safe and non-traumatizing to others. It restores your sense of equilibrium, at least temporarily, and over time can strengthen relationships and restore inner peace.

You may find this chart a handy guide.

Potentially Damaging Expression	Restorative Expression
Thinking about your guilt a lot but never speaking it out loud.	Speaking your guilt out loud whenever you're feeling it strongly.
Telling a child or vulnerable person a secret inappropriate for them to hear.	Discussing your guilty feelings or secret with an adult who is a good sounding board and can help you decide who else it would be appropriate for you to tell.
Blaming others for whatever it is you feel guilty about.	Taking responsibility for your own feelings and actions. Allowing others to take responsibility for theirs. Working to get to the core of your guilty feelings.

Snapping at, being passive-aggressive with, or avoiding others because of your guilt.	Practicing owning and sharing your feelings of guilt honestly and appropriately.
Taking part in harmful behaviors (overusing alcohol or drugs or other addictive behaviors, extreme risk-taking, self-harm) as a way of either escaping feelings of guilt or punishing yourself.	If you feel this impulse, seeing a counselor instead. If it's an emergency, calling 911
Telling yourself or others that there's nothing you can do to change what happened, so it's best not to bring it up.	Acting with intention to express your guilt fully and also to seek forgiveness and make amends, when necessary.
Withholding yourself from others (physically, emotionally, socially) because you feel unworthy of love and intimacy.	Opening yourself fully to others because you and those you care about deserve a whole, meaningful life.

WHITE LIES AND SECRETS

Is it ever OK to keep secrets?

Here's a good rule of thumb: If you're feeling guilty, that means you need to express your guilt. You may or may not need to share it with those most directly affected, however. Start with an outsider, discuss who else you should maybe open up to, then see how you feel. If you still feel guilty, that means you have more sharing to do.

There is a quote attributed to the ancient poet Rumi:

"Before you speak, let your words pass through three gates. At the first gate, ask yourself, 'Is it true?' At the second gate, ask yourself, 'Is it necessary?' At the third gate, ask yourself, 'Is it kind?'"

Speaking the truth (gate one) is necessary to reconcile your guilt (gate two). But if it's unnecessary and unkind to the listener, consider choosing a different listener first.

"White lies" as well as lying by omission are tactics we use to protect others. Sometimes these choices are wise. Sometimes, however, painful truths must be shared with people who will be hurt by them. Relationships are built on honesty and trust. When you withhold important truths from the people you care about—especially if those truths directly affect them in some way—you may be keeping the peace, but at what cost? If you feel it is unfair to someone to not share a secret with them, perhaps it is time to talk with them about it.

As you move forward in your grief journey, continue to use your guilt barometer to guide you. Ongoing, pronounced guilt demands ongoing expression. Sometimes sharing feelings or incidents of wrongdoing with the people closest to you is the only way to begin to reconcile them.

THE GIFTS OF VULNERABILITY

Sharing guilty feelings tends to make us feel really vulnerable. It can seem like we're revealing our very souls.

But one thing that I've learned as a companion to people in

deep grief is that getting more comfortable with vulnerability is essential to healing. In fact, mourning demands making yourself vulnerable to others. There's simply no way around it. You can't mourn and be invulnerable at the same time. Mourning guilt, in particular, makes us vulnerable because we're sharing our perceived wrongdoings, omissions, and sins. We're putting our worst foot forward, if you will, and we're opening ourselves to others to respond.

There's another way to look at it, though. Vulnerability is actually a superpower—one you can harness in this process of restoratively expressing your guilt. It's profound honesty. It's a way to build intimacy. And it's positive risk-taking. In expressing your guilt, you can become more at ease with being vulnerable. And when you become more at ease with vulnerability, you grow. You become a more open, genuine, congruent person.

To be congruent means to be the same on the outside as you are on the inside. Whatever you care most about in your heart of hearts, whatever values you hold and dreams you cherish, when you're congruent, you "live" those passions, loves, values, and dreams. You express them in every word and deed. You don't believe one thing and do another. Instead, you turn yourself inside-out, displaying your most tender, true self for all the world to see.

The Guilt of Grief

And the rewards of vulnerability are life's greatest gifts. Close friendships. Intimate love. The deep satisfaction of living out values. The forthright pursuit of dreams.

If your grief is complicated by guilt, and if you find yourself at an impasse on the journey to healing because of guilt, you actually have a wonderful opportunity. That opportunity is to practice vulnerability and work at becoming more comfortable with it. Not only can it heal your guilt and grief over time, it can deepen your experience of life in general.

MAKING THINGS RIGHT

Depending on the contributors to your guilty feelings, healing your guilt will also include some or all of the following:

Ask for forgiveness

Apologizing to whomever you feel you may have wronged, or to others affected by the loss, is often a freeing opportunity. Again, it doesn't necessarily matter if you did something that others consider "wrong." You can express your guilt or regret and apologize anyway. This is an essential step.

Make amends

There's a difference between apologizing and making amends: The former means saying you're sorry. The latter means making things right. Can you fix something you messed up? Can you make up for a mistake you made by offering a replacement of some kind? It's not always possible or appropriate to make amends, but when it is, it can help patch the hole you now feel.

Forgive yourself

Self-forgiveness is part of healing the guilt of your grief. You don't have to decide that you did nothing wrong or forget it ever happened. No. You simply need to acknowledge your humanity. Like all of us, you're a human being who makes mistakes and who sees more clearly in hindsight. This step, too, is essential.

Accept grace

Grace is the gift of goodness we didn't earn. Guilty feelings and grace can rub each other wrong. You may feel you don't deserve grace. Or you may feel even guiltier when good things come your way. But learning to forgive yourself and accept grace when it comes along are can't-miss waystations on the journey to healing.

A FINAL WORD

*"An exciting and inspiring future awaits you beyond the noise
in your mind, beyond the guilt, doubt, fear, shame, insecurity,
and heaviness of the past you carry around."*
— Debbie Ford

Just as you will always feel grief over this loss, you may
well continue to feel some guilt. After all, your guilt is part
of your grief! You wouldn't want to deaden yourself to
the capacity to feel guilt, anyway. It's still a normal human
emotion, and you shouldn't suppress your feelings or deny
yourself the full range of emotional responses. But through
intentional mourning, your healed guilt and grief can
become fully integrated parts of your life story.

So the goal moving forward isn't to be guilt-free but instead
guilt-healthy. In addition to understanding, embracing, and
restoratively expressing guilt, here are some tools for living a
guilt-healthy life.

Look forward
Guilt is backward-looking, but your ongoing life is today,
tomorrow, and the tomorrow after that. Cultivate hope for

the future by making plans with people you care about and taking small daily steps to do what matters most to you.

Practice self-compassion and self-love
Becoming your own best friend and advocate is a good way to prevent inappropriate levels of guilt, shame, and regret. Care for yourself physically, cognitively, emotionally, socially, and spiritually. Be kind to yourself first.

Build relationships
Close, honest, mutually supportive relationships help each of us maintain perspective about our judgments of ourselves and others. When kindness and empathy are strong, undue self-reproach tends to fall away.

When you know better, do better
In grief, you're probably learning all kinds of lessons. Use what you're learning to become a better person. Doing better will make you less susceptible to feelings of guilt, shame, and regret from here on.

Thank you for allowing me to be your companion on this painful journey through the guilt of grief. I hope you will return to this little guide often as you befriend and restoratively express your guilt.

I hope we meet one day.